## *About the author*

Neale Donald Walsch lives with his wife, Nancy, in southern Oregon. Together they have formed ReCreation, a non-profit foundation for personal growth and spiritual understanding with the goal of giving people back to themselves. Walsch lectures and hosts workshops throughout the USA to support and spread the messages contained in *Conversations with God*.

*Also by Neale Donald Walsch*

Conversations with God Book 1
Conversations with God Book 2
Conversations with God Book 3

# MEDITATIONS
# FROM
# CONVERSATIONS
# WITH GOD
## Book 1

### Neale Donald Walsch

Hodder & Stoughton

First published in Great Britain in 1997
by Hodder and Stoughton
A division of Hodder Headline PLC

The right of Neale Donald Walsch to be identified as the Author
of the Work has been asserted by him in accordance with the
Copyright, Designs and Patents Act 1988.

10 9 8 7 6 5 4 3 2 1

A CIP catalogue record for this title is available
from the British Library

ISBN 0 340 76595 X

Printed and bound in Great Britain by
Caledonian International Book Manufacturing, Ltd

Hodder and Stoughton
A division of Hodder Headline PLC
338 Euston Road
London NW1 3BH

# *Prologue*

When I was a child, my mother used to say, "God is always with you. God is your best friend." Of course, I believed her. She was, after all, my mother. It never occurred to me that she might not be speaking from her own experience. It never occurred to me that my mother may not have felt God's actual presence in *her* everyday life.

But as I grew older, *I* began to have doubts. I never doubted my mother's faith, but I began to wonder about its source. I had never had any direct experience of God in *my* life, and for someone who was "always with me," God was remarkably non-present. I never stopped believing in the existence of God, mind you. I just didn't quite get that God was even aware of—much less interested—in me.

Then in February 1992 I had an experience that changed all that. That was the month in which God began to speak to me. Personally. We entered, in fact, into a rather extensive dialogue. Lasting one full year, our exchanges became a book. We called it *Conversations with God*. Our conversation quenched in me an enormous thirst, satisfied in me an incredible hunger. And I hoped that by sharing it, it could do the same for others.

We have been searching for the God of our heart for a very long time. The God I met in my conversation was not a God to fear, but a God of unconditional and unlimited love. A God of deep compassion and understanding. A God of wonderful humor who takes pure delight in the joyful celebration of life. This is a God offering friendship, not lordship—and asking, in return, for friendship, not worship.

That is the God I would like all of us to know. And the wisdom of that kind God is the wisdom I wish we could live each day. These meditations offer a chance to do just that. Taken from the pages of *Conversations with God*, these words have been very helpful, very meaningful, and very inspiring to me.

I invite you to open this book each morning and embrace the day's thought. Meditate on its meaning. Then seek to bring that meaning into your life as you go about your day. At the close of the day, open this book again, turning to the page with which you began your morning. Read once more the words for the day. Take a moment to reflect on the hours just past, and the new context within which the words may be considered. Then close the book with thanks. And, if it feels good to do so, write in your journal what has come to you from this process. Put down whatever comes to your mind.

In this way you can use the daily meditations here to begin your own conversation with God.

—Neale Donald Walsch
Ashland, Oregon
May 1997

# Meditations from
# *Conversations with God*

## book 1

*January 1*

It is not God's function to create or
uncreate the circumstances and
conditions of your life. God
created You, in the image and
likeness of God. You have created
the rest.

p. 13

*January 2*

Do the deed that you want to have
the new thought about. Then say
the words that you want to have
your new thought about. Do this
often enough and you'll train the
mind to think a new way.

p. 164

## January 3

I have always been here to help
you, I am here now. You don't
have to find the answers on your
own. You never had to.

p. 66

*January 4*

A true Master is not the one with
the most students, but one who
creates the most Masters.

p. 114

*January 5*

Your ideas about Right and Wrong
are just that—ideas. They are the
thoughts which form the shape
and create the substance of Who
You Are. There would be only one
reason to change any of these;
only one purpose in making an
alteration; if you are not happy
with who you are.

p. 62

## *January 6*

Life is eternal. You are immortal.
You never do die. You simply
change form.

p. 193

*January* 7

God's greatest moment is the
moment you realize you need no
God.

p. 114

## January 8

Let your love propel your beloveds
into the world—and into the full
experience of who they are. In this
will you have truly loved.

p. 115

## January 9

If you have caught yourself in an
ungodly act as a result of doing
what is best for you, the confusion
is not in having put yourself first,
but rather in misunderstanding
what is best for you.

p. 132

*January 10*

Treating others with love does not
necessarily mean allowing others
to do as they wish.

p. 132

## January 11

God asks only that you include
yourself among those you love.

p. 132

## January 12

If there were such a thing as sin,
this would be it: to allow yourself
to become what you are because
of the experience of others.

p. 62

*January 13*

If your values serve you, hold to them. Argue for them. Fight to defend them. Yet seek to fight in a way which harms no one. Harm is not a necessary ingredient in healing.

p. 62

*January 14*

The soul—your soul—knows all
there is to know all the time. There
is nothing hidden to it, nothing
unknown. Yet knowing is not
enough. The soul seeks to
experience.

p. 22

## January 15

You can know yourself to be
generous, but unless you do
something which displays
generosity, you have nothing but a
concept. You can know yourself to
be kind, but unless you do
someone a kindness, you have
nothing but an idea about yourself.

p. 22

*January 16*

The first thing to understand about
the universe is that no condition is
"good" or "bad." It just is. So stop
making value judgments.

p. 79

The first step in changing anything
is to know and accept that you
have chosen it to be what it is. If
you can't accept this on a personal
level, agree to it through your
understanding that we are all one.
Seek then to create change not
because a thing is wrong, but
because it no longer makes an
accurate statement of who you are.

*January 18*

My purpose in creating you, My
spiritual offspring, was for Me to
know Myself as God. I have no
way to do that save through you.

p. 26

*January 19*

By your decisions you paint a
portrait of Who You Are.

p. 154

*January 20*

No one who has attained mastery
is dull. Unusual, perhaps.
Extraordinary, perhaps. But never
dull.

p. 78

## January 21

Have you ever seen anything more perfect than a snowflake? Its intricacy, its design, its symmetry, its conformity to itself and originality from all else are all a mystery. You wonder at the miracle of this awesome display of nature. Yet if I can do this with a single snowflake, what think you I can do—have done—with the universe?

p. 43

## January 22

I will do nothing for you that you
will not do for your Self. That is
the law and the prophets.

p. 50

## January 23

You cannot experience yourself as
what you are until you've
encountered what you are not.
This is the purpose of the theory of
relativity, and all physical life. It is
by that which you are not that you
yourself are defined.

p. 27

## January 24

I suggest that it is your judgments which keep you from joy, and your expectations which make you unhappy.

p. 108

## January 25

Masters are those who have chosen only love. In every instance. In every moment. In every circumstance.

p. 57

## January 26

I invite you to a new form of
communication with God. A two-
way communication. In truth, it is
you who have invited Me. For I
have come to you, in this form,
right now, in answer to your call.

p. 7

*January* 27

You must first learn to honor and
cherish and love your Self.

p. 126

*January 28*

Every heart which earnestly asks,
Which is the path to God? is
shown.

p. 94

*January 29*

The process of prayer becomes
much easier when, rather than
having to believe that God will
always say yes to every request,
one understands intuitively that the
request itself is not necessary.

p. 13

## January 30

When you have a thought that is
not in alignment with your higher
vision, change to a new thought,
then and there. When you say a
thing that is out of alignment with
your grandest idea, make a note
not to say something like that
again.

p. 78

## January 31

You are goodness and mercy and
compassion and understanding.
You are peace and joy and light.
You are forgiveness and patience,
strength and courage, a helper in
time of need, a comforter in time
of sorrow, a healer in time of
injury, a teacher in times of
confusion.

p. 121

*February 1*

God is the energy you call
imagination. God is creation. God
is first thought. And God is last
experience. And God is everything
in between.

p. 198

*February 2*

Your teachers have told you of an
angry God, a jealous God, a God
who needs to be needed. And that
is not a God at all, but a neurotic
substitute for that which would be
a deity.

p. 114

*February 3*

It is your first nature to be
unconditionally loving.

p. 78

*February 4*

I will do nothing for you that you
will not do for your Self. That is
the law of the prophets. The world
is in the condition it is in because
of you, and the choices you have
made—or failed to make. The
Earth is in the shape it's in because
of you, and the choices you have
made—or failed to make. Your
own life is the way it is because of
you, and the choices you have
made—or failed to make.

p. 50

*February 5*

Bless every person and condition,
and give thanks Thus you affirm
the perfection of God's creation—
and show your faith in it. For
nothing happens by accident in
God's world, and there is no such
thing as coincidence. Nor is the
world buffeted by random choice,
or something you call fate!

p. 114

*February 6*

There is only what serves you, and
what does not. The terms "right"
and "wrong" are relative terms.

p. 162

*February* 7

Allow each soul to walk its path.

p. 47

*February 8*

There is nothing scary about life if
you are not attached to results.

p. 110

## *February 9*

You are, have always been and will always be, a divine part of the divine whole, a member of the body. That is why the act of rejoining the Whole, of returning to God, is called remembrance. You actually choose to re-member Who You Really Are, or to join together with the various parts of you to experience the all of you—which is to say, the All of Me.

p. 28

*February 10*

Your perception of ultimate reality
is more limited than you thought,
and Truth is more unlimited than
you can imagine.

p. 197

## February 11

This is the second great illusion of
man: that the outcome of life is in
doubt. It is this doubt about
ultimate outcome that has created
your greatest enemy, which is fear.
For if you doubt outcome, then
you must doubt the creator—you
must doubt God.

p. 14

*February 12*

I have given you nothing shameful,
least of all your very body, and its
functions.

p. 208

*February 13*

Ultimately all Spirit renounces what
is not real, and nothing in the life
you lead is real, save your
relationship with Me.

p. 100

*February 14*

At the critical juncture in all human
relationships, there is only one
question:
What would love do now?

p. 130

*February 15*

There are those who say you must
overcome your desires. I say you
must simply change them. The first
practice feels like a rigorous
discipline, the second, a joyful
exercise.

p. 159

*February 16*

You're setting your sights too low.
Broaden the scope of your
horizons. Extend the depth of your
vision. See more in you than you
think there is to be seen.

p. 142

*February* 17

You are the deepest wisdom and
the highest truth; the greatest
peace and the grandest love. You
are these things. And in moments
of your life you have known
yourself as these things. Choose
now to know yourself as these
things always.

p. 87

*February 18*

People assume that if God were to
talk directly with you, God would
not sound like the fella next door.

p. 68

*February 19*

Stop making judgments against
yourself.

p. 71

## February 20

The world exists the way it exists—
just as a snowflake exists the way
it exists—quite by design. You
have created it that way—just as
you have created your life exactly
as it is.

p. 49

*February 21*

Your body, your mind and your
soul (spirit) are one. In this, you
are a microcosm of Me—the
Divine All, the Holy Everything,
the Sum and the Substance.

p. 197

*February 22*

The deepest secret is that life is not
a process of discovery, but a
process of creation. You are not
discovering yourself, but creating
yourself anew. Seek, therefore, not
to find out who you are, seek to
determine who you want to be.

p. 21

## February 23

This is the root of every problem you experience in your life—you do not consider yourself worthy enough to be spoken to by God. Good heavens, how can you ever expect to hear my voice if you don't imagine yourself to be deserving enough to even be spoken to?

p. 162

*February 24*

One day, if you have a great deal
of courage, you will experience a
world where making love is
considered better than making war.
On that day will you rejoice.

p. 109

*February 25*

Life will "take off" for you . . .
when you choose for it to . . . you
must believe the promise and live
it. You must live the promise of
God.

p. 75

*February 26*

Stop questioning your motives
(you do it incessantly) and let's get
on with it.

p. 70

## February 27

You are evolving, you are
becoming. And you are using your
relationship with everything to
decide what you are becoming.
This is the job you came here to
do. This is the joy of creating self.
Of knowing self. Of becoming,
consciously, what you wish to be.

p. 126

*February 28*

Come to Me along the path of your
heart, not through a journey of
your mind. You will never find Me
in your mind.

*February 29*

Would you not be better off to think the thoughts you want to think, than those of others? Are you not better armed with creative thoughts than with reactive thoughts?

p. 165

## *March 1*


You say it is difficult to walk the
path of Christ, to follow the
teachings of the Buddha, to hold
the light of Krishna, to be a Master.
Yet I tell you this: It is far more
difficult to deny Who You Are than
to accept it.

p. 86

## *March 2*

If humans do not change some of
their Sponsoring Thoughts,
humankind could doom itself to
extinction.

p. 164

## March 3

Worry is the activity of a mind
which does not understand its
connection with Me.

## March 4

No prayer—and a prayer is
nothing more than a fervent
statement of what is so—goes
unanswered.

p. 12

## March 5

It is when the going gets tough that
you so often forget Who You Are,
and the tools I have given you for
creating the life that you would
choose.

p. 116

## March 6

The job of the soul, of course, is to
cause us to choose the grandeur—
to select the best of who you are—
without condemning that which
you do not select.

p. 84

*March* 7

If a thing is obviously right, do it.

p. 47

## March 8

Envy not success, nor pity failure,
for you know not what is success
or failure in the soul's reckoning.

p. 33

## March 9

Relationships are constantly
challenging, constantly calling you
to create, express and experience
higher and higher aspects of
yourself, grander and grander
visions of yourself, ever more
magnificent versions of yourself.

p. 121

## March 10

Everlasting perspective helps you
keep things in their proper light.

p. 116

## March 11

It's important now, it's time now,
to change your mind about some
things. This is what evolution is all
about.

p. 168

*March 12*

The person who has the "faith to move mountains," and dies six weeks later, has moved mountains for six weeks. That may have been enough for him.

p. 80

*March 13*

There is perfection in the process, and all life arises out of choice. It is not appropriate to interfere with choice, nor to question it. It is particularly inappropriate to condemn it.

p. 47

*March 14*

A society living in fear very often—
actually, inevitably—produces in
form that which it fears most.

p. 55

# March 15

Everything in life is holy.

p. 68

## March 16

Killing can never be justified as a
means of expressing anger,
releasing hostility, "righting a
wrong" or punishing an offender.

p. 151

## March 17

By their decisions your religions
have created lasting, indelible
impressions. By their decisions
your societies have produced their
self-portraits, too. Are you pleased
with these pictures? Are these the
impressions you wish to make?

p. 154

## March 18

This is My plan for you. This is My
ideal: that I should become
realized through you.

p. 43

*March 19*

You must live the promise of God.

p. 75

## March 20

You are in a partnership with God.
We share an eternal covenant. My
promise to you is to always give
you what you ask. Your promise is
to ask.

p. 73

## *March 21*

I have established Laws in the
universe that make it possible for
you to have—to create—exactly
what you choose. These Laws
cannot be violated, nor can they be
ignored.

p. 75

## March 22

You will never disserve your relationship—nor anyone—by seeing more in another than they are showing you. For there is more there. Much more. It is only their fear that stops them from showing you.

p. 142

## March 23

Health will improve almost at once
when worrying ends.

p. 188

## March 24

If you think your life is about doingness, you do not understand what you are about. Your soul doesn't care what you do for a living—and when your life is over, neither will you. Your soul cares only about what you're being while you're doing whatever you're doing.

p. 170

## March 25

The question is not, why start off
on such a path? You have already
started off. You did so with the first
beat of your heart. The question is:
Do I wish to walk this path
consciously, or unconsciously?

p. 156

*March 26*

So long as you entertain the notion
that there is something or someone
else out there "doing it" to you,
you disempower yourself to do
anything about it.

p. 36

## *March* 27

Do not feel abandoned. I am
always with you.

p. 210

## *March 28*

Desire is the beginning of all creation. It is first thought. It is a grand feeling within the soul. It is God, choosing what next to create.

p. 65

## *March 29*

You don't have a clear focus;
you're not really sure what's true
for you. And the universe is just a
big Xerox machine. It simply
produces multiple copies of your
thoughts. Now there's only one
way to change all that. You have to
change your thought about it.

p. 163

## *March 30*

It might not be a bad goal in your
life to know the highest part of
your Self, and to stay centered in
that.

p. 126

*March 31*

Expectations ruin relationships.

p. 142

## April 1

Do you imagine that God does not
enjoy a good joke? Is it your
knowing that God is without
humor? I tell you, God invented
humor.

p. 60

## April 2

Your happy destiny is unavoidable.
You cannot not be "saved." There
is no hell except not knowing this.

p. 115

## April 3

The Master knows intuitively that
passion is the path. It is the way to
self-realization. Even in earthly
terms it can be fairly sad that if you
have a passion for nothing, you
have no life at all.

## April 4

You have no obligation in relationship. You have only opportunity. Opportunity, not obligation, is the cornerstone of religion, the basis of spirituality. So long as you see it the other way around, you will have missed the point.

p. 137

## April 5

You are wont to rush to judgment,
to call a thing "wrong" or "bad" or
"not enough," rather than to bless
what you do not choose.

*April 6*

You are in the process of
experiencing yourself by creating
yourself anew in every single
moment. As am I. Through you.

p. 75

*April* 7

Sometimes, when a person is really
deeply asleep, you have to shake
him a little.

p. 191

*April 8*

There is no need to recriminate
yourself. Simply notice what
you've been choosing and choose
again.

p. 119

*April 9*

Every prayer—every thought,
every feeling, every statement—is
creative. To the extent that it is
fervently held as truth, to that
degree will it be made manifest in
your experience.

p. 12

*April 10*

You can choose to be a person
who has resulted simply from what
has happened, or from what you
have chosen to be and do about
what has happened.

p. 122

## April 11

Call not a thing calamity, nor
joyous event, until you decide, or
witness, how it is used.

p. 33

*April 12*

Your soul seeks the highest
feeling. It seeks to experience—to
be—perfect love.

p. 85

*April 13*

The reason that the true Master
does not complain is that the true
Master is not suffering, but simply
experiencing a set of circumstances
that you *would call insufferable*.

p. 107

*April 14*

You have nothing to learn about
relationships. You have only to
demonstrate what you already
know.

p. 121

*April 15*

True Masters are those who have
chosen to make a life, rather than a
living.

p. 176

## April 16

God is in the sadness and in
laughter. In the bitter and the
sweet.

p. 60

*April 17*

There are those who say that to
know God you must overcome all
earthly passions. Yet to understand
and accept them is enough. What
you resist persists. What you look
at disappears.

p. 100

## April 18

I will not leave you, I cannot leave
you, for you are My creation and
My product, My daughter and My
son, My purpose and My . . . Self.
Call on me, therefore, wherever
and whenever you are separate
from the peace that I am.

p. 211

*April 19*

Fear is the opposite of everything
you are.

p. 188

## April 20

You cannot lie to yourself. Your mind knows the truth of your thoughts.

p. 11

*April 21*

This is both the goal and the glory of God: that His subjects shall be no more, and that all shall know God not as the unattainable, but as the unavoidable.

p. 115

*April 22*

When you achieve certain states of
being over a long period of time,
success in what you are doing in
the world is very difficult to avoid.

p. 176

## *April 23*

There is no such thing as karmic
debt.

p. 204

*April 24*

Sex is an extraordinary expression
of love—love of another, love of
self, love of life. You ought to
therefore love it!

*April 25*

Do not dismantle the house, but
look at each brick, and replace
those which appear broken, which
no longer support the structure.

p. 62

## April 26

In the moment of your total
knowing, you, too, will feel as I do
always: totally joyful, loving,
accepting, blessing and grateful.
These are the Five Attitudes of
God.

p. 65

*April* 27

Only when you say "I did this" can
you find the power to change it.

p. 36

*April 28*

You have a right to your joy; Seek
it! Find it!

p. 186

*April 29*

Are you not being allowed to
experience everything? The tears,
the joy, the pain, the gladness, the
exaltation, the massive depression,
the win, the lose, the draw? What
more is there?

p. 158

*April 30*

My teachers have all come with the same message. Not "I am holier than thou," but "you are as holy as am I."

p. 127

## May 1

The purpose of relationship is not
to have another who might
complete you; but to have another
with whom you might share your
completeness.

p. 123

*May 2*

Your world would not be in its
present condition were you to
have simply listened to your
experience. The result of your not
listening to your experience is that
you keep reliving it, over and over
again.

p. 5

*May 3*

If you think you are right about
everything, who needs to talk with
God?

p. 7

*May 4*

Why not simply acknowledge the truth when you hear it, and move towards it?

p. 119

## May 5

My messages will come in a
hundred forms, at a thousand
moments, across a million years.
You cannot miss them if you truly
listen. You cannot ignore them
once truly heard.

p. 6

## May 6

There is a divine purpose behind
everything, and therefore a divine
presence in everything.

p. 60

*May* 7

Some people don't like to be
awakened. Most do not. Most
would rather sleep.

p. 191

*May 8*

You can't go wrong. It's not part of
the plan. There's no way not to get
where you are going. There's no
way to miss your destination. If
God is your target, you're in luck,
because God is so big, you can't
miss.

## May 9

Do not condemn, therefore, all that
you would call bad in the world.
Rather, ask yourself, what about
this have you judged bad, and
what, if anything, you wish to do
to change it.

p. 32

## May 10

If you are God's equal, that means
nothing is being done to you—and
all things are created by you. There
can be no more victims and no
more villians—only outcomes of
your thought about a thing.

p. 75

*May 11*

Your will for you is God's will for
you.

p. 13

*May 12*

Each circumstance is a gift, and in
each experience is hidden a
treasure.

p. 33

## May 13

Love is the ultimate reality. It is the
only. The all. The feeling of love is
your experience of God.

p. 56

## May 14

Do you want your life to truly take off? Then change your idea about it. About you. Think, speak and act as the God you are.

p. 76

## *May 15*

Listen to me in the truth of your
soul. Listen to me in the feelings of
your heart. Listen to me in the
quiet of your mind.

p. 210

## May 16

Well, if God can't inspire you, who in hell can?

p. 88

## May 17

I have never set down a "right" or "wrong," a "do" or a "don't." To do so would be to strip you completely of your greatest gift— the opportunity to do as you please, and experience the results of that.

p. 39

*May 18*

We dare not solve all the
problems, or there will be nothing
left for us to do.

p. 48

## May 19

Go first to your Highest Thought
about yourself. Imagine the you
that you would be if you lived that
thought every day.

p. 77

## May 20

Judge not, and neither condemn,
for you know not why a thing
occurs, nor to what end.

p. 38

## *May 21*

The work of the soul is to wake
yourself up. The work of God is to
wake everybody else up.

p. 142

## May 22

If you choose evolution—the
evolution of your soul—you won't
produce that by the worldy
activities of your body.

p. 170

## May 23

For goodness' sake, don't destroy
sexual innocence and pleasure and
the purity of the fun, the joy, by
misusing sex. Don't use it for
power or hidden purpose; for ego
gratification or domination; or any
purpose other than the purest joy
and the highest ecstasy, given and
shared—which is love.

p. 206

## May 24

You are the creator of your reality,
and life can show up no other way
for you than that way in which you
think it will.

p. 52

*May 25*

There is nothing you cannot be.
There is nothing you cannot do.
There is nothing you cannot have.
What other kind of promise would
you have God make? Would you
believe Me if I promised you less?

p. 44

## *May 26*

When you choose the action love
sponsors, then will you do more
than survive, then will you do
more than win, then will you do
more than succeed. Then will
you experience the full glory of
Who You Really Are, and who you
can be.

p. 19

## May 27

Do Me a favor and don't try to
contain Me. By the way, do
yourself the same favor.

p. 88

## May 28

You have come here to work out
an individual plan for your own
salvation. Yet salvation does not
mean saving yourself from the
snares of the devil. There is no
such thing as the devil, and hell
does not exist. You are saving
yourself from the oblivion of non-
realization.

p. 51

## May 29

Every one of My messengers has
been defiled. Far from gaining
glory, they have gained nothing
but heartache. Are you willing?
Does your heart ache to tell the
truth about Me?

p. 145

*May 30*

I gave to each of the countless
parts of Me (to all of my spirit
children) the same power to create
which I have as the whole.

p. 25

*May 31*

It is your first nature to be
unconditionally loving. It is your
second nature to choose to express
your first nature, your true nature,
consciously.

p. 78

## June 1

Words are merely utterances:
noises that stand for feelings,
thoughts and experience. They are
symbols. Signs. Insignias. They are
not Truth. They are not the real
thing.

p. 4

## *June 2*

Most people enter into
relationships with an eye toward
what they can get out of them,
rather than what they can put into
them.

p. 122

*June 3*

Feeling guilty is a learned
response.

p. 119

## June 4

Fear is the other end of love. It is
the primal polarity.

p. 57

*June 5*

If you believe that God is some
omnipotent Being who hears all
prayers, says "yes" to some, "no"
to others, and "maybe, but not
now" to the rest, you are mistaken.
By what rule of thumb would God
decide?

p. 13

I do not communicate by words
alone. In fact, rarely do I do so. My
most common form of
communication is through feeling.

## *June* 7

The world is in the condition it's in because the world is full of sleepwalkers.

p. 191

## June 8

I will bring you the exact right
thoughts, words or feelings, at any
given moment, suited precisely to
the purpose at hand.

p. 6

## June 9

I tell you this: you are your own
rule-maker. You set the guidelines.
And you decide how well you
have done; how well you are
doing.

p. 41

## June 10

When you thank God in advance
for that which you choose to
experience in your reality, you, in
effect, acknowledge that it is there.

p. 11

## June 11

Your first relationship must be with yourself.

p. 126

*June 12*

For thousands of years people
have disbelieved the promises of
God for the most extraordinary
reason: they were too good to be
true.

p. 44

## June 13

Begin at once to imagine life the
way you want it to be—and move
into that. Check every thought,
word and action that does not fall
into harmony with that. Move
away from those.

p. 78

## June 14

All human actions are motivated at their deepest level by one of two emotions—fear or love.

p. 15

*June 15*

It is not a question of learning, but
of remembering.

p. 43

## June 16

You can define present conditions
and circumstances as what they
truly are: temporary and temporal.

p. 116

*June 17*

I want for you what you want for
you. Nothing more, nothing less. I
don't sit here and make a
judgment, request by request,
whether something should be
granted you. My law is the law of
cause and effect, not the law of
"We'll See."

p. 117

*June 18*

From the highest mountain it has
been shouted, in the lowest pure
its whisper has been heard.
Through the corridors of all human
experience has this Truth been
echoed: Love is the answer.

p. 58

*June 19*

Worry is just about the worst form
of mental activity there is . . . Worry
is pointless. It is wasted mental
energy.

p. 188

## June 20

It is not in the action of another,
but in your re-action, that your
salvation will be found.

p. 127

## *June 21*

I will speak to you if you will
listen. I will come to you if you
will invite Me. I will show you then
that I have always been there. All
ways.

p. 58

*June* 22

I tell you, you can speak to Me as
you would speak with your best
friend.

p. 60

*June 23*

Not to decide is to decide.

p. 50

## June 24

Marriage is a sacrament. But not
because of its sacred obligations.
Rather, because of its unequaled
opportunity.

p. 138

## June 25

The world will need many voices
to speak the words of truth and
healing for which millions long.
The world will need many hearts
joined together in the work of the
soul, and prepared to do the work
of God. Can you honestly claim
that you are not aware of this?

p. 144

## June 26

Hear Me, everywhere. Whenever
you have a question, simply know
that I have answered it already.
Then open your eyes to your
world.

p. 210

## *June* 27

There are no coincidences in the
universe.

p. 58

*June 28*

All conditions are temporary.

p. 79

## June 29

So what is your intention now? Do
you intend to prove your theory
that life seldom brings you what
you choose? Or do you intend to
demonstrate Who You Are and
Who I Am?

p. 119

## June 30

I tell you there is no such
experience after death as you have
constructed in your fear-based
theologies.

p. 41

## July 1

I do not make a judgment about
the creations that you conjure. I
simply empower you to conjure
more—and more and more and
more.

p. 118

## July 2

Your saying you want a thing only
works to produce that precise
experience—wanting—in your
reality. The correct prayer is
therefore never a prayer of
supplication, but a prayer of
gratitude.

p. 11

## July 3

Are you going to be in a place
called fear, or in a place called
love? Where are you—and where
are you coming from—as you
encounter life?

p. 172

## July 4

How can you be a creative being if
I am dictating what you shall be,
do and have? My joy is in your
freedom, not your compliance.

p. 166

*July 5*

When life is lived from a
standpoint of damage control or
optimum advantage, the true
benefit of life is forfeited. The
opportunity is lost. The chance is
missed. For a life lived thusly is a
life lived from fear.

p. 130

*July 6*

Do you not see that I could just as easily work through your imagination as anything else?

p. 6

*July* 7

Obedience is not creation, and
thus can never produce salvation.
Obedience is a response, while
creation is pure choice, undictated,
unrequired.

p. 175

## July 8

When you are in your God space,
you know and understand that all
you are now experiencing is
temporary. I tell you that heaven
and earth shall pass away, but you
shall not.

p. 116

## July 9

Bring to the space of your
experience the highest and best
idea you ever had about you.

p. 66

## July 10

Mine is always your Highest
Thought, your Clearest Word, your
Grandest Feeling. Anything less is
from another source.

p. 4

## July 11

I have heard the crying of your
heart. I have seen the searching of
your soul.

p. 58

*July 12*

No one will judge you ever, for
why, and how, could God judge
God's own creation and call it bad?

p. 41

## July 13

You have brought your Self to the
relative world so that you might
have the tools with which to know
and experience Who You Really
Are. Who You Are is who you
create yourself to be in relationship
to all the rest of it.

p. 126

## July 14

Thoughts rooted in fear will produce one kind of manifestation on the physical plane, thoughts rooted in love will produce another. The masters are those who have chosen only love. In every instant. In every moment. In every circumstance.

p. 57

*July 15*

Nothing happens to you or
through you that is not for your
own highest good.

p. 174

## July 16

Belief in God produces belief in God's greatest gift—unconditional love—and God's greatest promise—unlimited potential.

p. 44

## *July* 17

There are a million aspects to Me.
A billion. A trillion. You see? There
is the profane and the profound,
the lesser and the larger, the
hollow and the holy, the ghastly
and the Godly.

p. 173

*July 18*

This is the goal of your soul, this is
its purpose: to fully realize itself
while in the body; to become the
embodiment of all that it really is.

p. 43

## July 19

Do not what you are obliged to do,
but what you have an opportunity
to do.

p. 145

*July 20*

The soul leads you to the right and
perfect opportunities for you to
experience exactly what you had
planned to experience. What you
actually experience is up to you.

p. 174

## July 21

Fear is the energy which contracts,
closes down, draws in, runs, hides,
hoards, harms. Love is the energy
which expands, opens up, sends
out, stays, reveals, shares, heals.

p. 19

*July 22*

The people who make a living
doing what they love are the
people who insist on doing so.

p. 169

## July 23

Suffering has nothing to do with
events, but with one's reaction to
them. What's happening is merely
what's happening. How you feel
about it is another matter.

p. 105

*July 24*

The actions of the body were
meant to be reflections of a state of
being, not attempts to attain a state
of being.

p. 185

## July 25

The way to reduce the pain which
you associate with earthly
experiences and events—both
yours and those of others—is to
change the way you behold them.
You cannot change the outer
event, so you must change the
inner experience.

p. 3

*July 26*

We make real that to which we
pay attention.

p. 107

*July* 27

Do you imagine this is too big a problem for Me to solve? I see, so it's a matter of faith. You don't question My ability, you merely doubt My desire.

p. 117

## July 28

The voice within is the loudest
voice with which I speak, because
it is the closest to you. It is the
voice which tells you whether
everything else is true or false,
right or wrong, good or bad as you
have defined it. It is the radar that
sets the course, steers the ship,
guides the journey if you but let it.

p. 20

*July 29*

The purpose of a relationship is to
decide what part of yourself you'd
like to see "show up," not what
part of another you can capture
and hold.

p. 122

## July 30

When you have a thought that is
not in alignment with your higher
vision, change to a new thought,
then and there. When you say a
thing which is out of alignment
with your grandest idea, make a
note not to say something like that
again. When you do a thing which
is misaligned with your best
intention, decide to make that the
last time.

*July 31*

What your body is doing is a
reflection of what your life is
about.

p. 186

*August 1*

You are not on this planet to
produce anything with your body.
You on are on this planet to
produce something with your soul.
Your body is simply and merely
the tool of your soul.

p. 172

*August 2*

The more you are, the more you
can become, and the more you can
become, the more you can yet be.

p. 20

*August 3*

If you want to know what's true for
you about something, look to how
you're feeling about it. Feelings are
sometimes difficult to discover—
and often even more difficult to
acknowledge. Yet hidden in your
deepest feelings is your highest
truth.

p. 3

*August 4*

You'll get as many chances as you
want and need. You can come
back again and again and again. If
you do get to the next step, if you
evolve to the next level, it's
because you want to, not because
you have to.

p. 149

## August 5

I will continue sending you the
same messages over and over
again, throughout the millenia and
to whatever corner of the universe
you occupy. Endlessly will I send
you My messages, until you have
received them and held them
close, calling them your own.

p. 5

## August 6

It takes great courage to announce
oneself as a man of God. You
understand, the world will much
more readily accept you as
virtually anything else.

p. 145

## *August* 7

Next time, decide to act before you think.

p. 168

*August 8*

In the true order of things one
does not do something in order to
be happy—one is happy, and,
hence, does something.

p. 185

*August 9*

Do you think there is a word I
have not heard? A sight I have not
seen? A sound I do not know? Is it
your thought that I despise some
of these, while I love the others? I
tell you, I despise nothing. None of
it is repulsive to Me. It is life, and
life is the gift; the unspeakable
treasure; the holy of holies.

p. 60

## August 10

All the "bad" things that happen
are of your choosing. The mistake
is not in choosing them, but in
calling them bad.

p. 36

*August 11*

The function of the soul is to
indicate its desire, not impose it.

p. 175

Your life work is a statement of
Who You Are. If it is not, then why
are you doing it?

*August 13*

You cannot experience yourself as
what you are until you've
encountered what you are not.

p. 27

## August 14

Seek to change those things—or
support others who are changing
those things—which no longer
reflect your highest sense of Who
You are.

p. 38

## August 15

Doing is a function of the body.
Being is a function of the soul.

p. 170

If you don't like what you've just created, choose again. My job, as God, is to always give you that opportunity.

p. 118

## *August* 17

There is only one purpose for all of life, and that is for you and all that lives to experience fullest glory. Everything else you say, think or do is attendant to that function.

p. 20

## August 18

If you want guarantees in life, then you don't want life. You want rehearsals for a script that's already been written.

p. 141

*August 19*

There is no coincidence, and
nothing happens "by accident."

p. 52

*August 20*

You misunderstand your power. I
tell you this: Your life proceeds out
of your intentions for it.

p. 118

*August 21*

The soul conceives, the mind
creates, the body experiences. The
circle is complete. The soul then
knows itself in its own experience.

p. 196

*August* 22

There's a difference between being
and doing, and most people have
placed their emphasis on the latter.

p. 196

*August 23*

Now, having seen the differences
between where you are and where
you want to be, begin to change—
consciously change—your
thoughts, words and actions to
match your grandest vision.

p. 77

*August* 24

Move into communion with the
souls of others, and their purpose,
their intention, will be clear to you.

p. 47

*August 25*

The moral codes, religious
constrictions, social taboos and
emotional conventions you have
placed around sex have made it
virtually impossible for you to
celebrate your being.

p. 208

*August* 26

You may think this is easy, this Be
Who You Really Are business, but
it's the most challenging thing
you'll ever do in your life.

p. 148

## August 27

There is only one reason to do
anything: as a statement to the
universe of Who You Are.

p. 36

*August 28*

Remember to exercise extreme
judgment regarding what you call
"right" and "wrong."

p. 47

*August 29*

Are you willing to endure the
ridicule of your fellow human
beings? Are you prepared to give
up glory on Earth for the greater
glory of the soul fully realized?

p. 145

*August 30*

The spirit in you seeks that grand
moment when you have conscious
awareness of its wishes, and join in
joyful oneness with them.

p. 174

*August 31*

You are not discovering yourself,
but creating yourself anew. Seek,
therefore, not to find out who you
are, seek to determine who you
want to be.

p. 20

*September 1*

You call a life of complete freedom
"spiritual anarchy." I call it God's
great promise. It is only within the
context of this promise that God's
great plan can be completed.

p. 137

*September 2*

If, then, revelation is requested, it
cannot be had, for the act of asking
is a statement that it is not there.

p. 10

*September 3*

The act of resisting something is
the act of granting it life. . . . the
more you resist, the more you
make it real—whatever it is you
are resisting.

p. 102

*September 4*

You cannot disembark from the journey. You embarked before you were born. Your birth is simply a sign that the journey has begun.

p. 156

*September 5*

The Highest Thought is always that
thought which contains joy. The
Clearest Words are those words
which contain truth. The Grandest
Feeling is that feeling which you
call love.

p. 5

*September 6*

All people are special, and all
moments are golden. There is no
person, and there is no time one
more special than another.

p. 6

*September* 7

You always get what you create,
and you are always creating.

p. 118

*September 8*

You cannot know God until you
stop telling yourself that you
already know God. You cannot
hear God until you stop thinking
that you've already heard God.

p. 8

*September 9*


If you knew Who You Are—that
you are the most magnificent, the
most remarkable, the most
splendid being God has ever
created—you would never fear.
For who could reject such
wondrous magnificence?

p. 16

*September 10*

When the body, mind and soul
create together, in harmony and in
unity, God is made flesh. Then
does the soul know itself in its
own experience. Then do the
heavens rejoice.

p. 175

*September 11*

Judge not that about which you
feel passionate. Simply notice it,
then see if it serves you, given who
and what you wish to be.

p. 100

*September 12*

Admit honestly to yourself and to
another exactly how you are
feeling.

p. 128

*September 13*

Inquire within, rather than without,
asking: "What part of my Self do I
wish to experience now in the face
of this calamity? What aspect of
being do I choose to call forth?"

p. 32

*September 14*

You have forgotten what it was
like to be loved without condition.
You do not remember the
experience of the love of God. And
so you try to imagine what God's
love must be like, based on what
you see of love in the world.

p. 17

*September 15*

The intention is for you not to fail.

p. 149

*September 16*

Some events you produce willfully, and some events you draw to you— more or less unconsciously. Some events are written off to "fate." Yet even "fate" can be an acronym for "from all thoughts everywhere." In other words, the consciousness of the planet.

p. 106

*September 1 7*

The answer is the answer you
cannot hear—for it leaves you
without guidelines and renders null
and void every agreement in the
moment you make it. The answer
is: You have no obligation. Neither
in relationship, nor in all of life.

p. 135

*September 18*

Seek not to make of your love a
glue that binds, but rather a
magnet that first attracts, then turns
around and repels, lest those who
are attracted begin to believe they
must stick to you to survive.

p. 115

*September 19*

I have created you—blessed you—
in the image and likeness of Me.

p. 95

*September 20*

The most difficult thing for people
to do is to hear their own soul.
(Notice that so few people do.)

p. 81

Sex is joy, and many of you have
made sex everything else but.

p. 207

*September* 22

You create, collectively and
individually, the life and times you
are experiencing, for the soul
purpose of evolving.

p. 37

*September 23*

That which you fear strongly you
will experience.

p. 54

*September 24*

I truly want what you truly want—
nothing different and nothing
more. Don't you see that is my
greatest gift to you?

p. 166

## September 25

See the Divine in a baby who
needs changing at 3 a.m. . . . in a
bill that needs paying by the first of
the month. Recognize the hand of
God in the illness that takes a
spouse, the job that's lost, the
child's fever, the parent's pain.
Now we are talking saintliness.

p. 115

*September 26*

If, now, there is something you
choose to experience in your life,
do not "want it"—choose it.

p. 180

*September* 27

You are already a God. You simply do not know it.

p. 202

*September 28*

Choosing to be God-like does not
mean that you choose to be a
martyr. And it certainly does not
mean you choose to be a victim.

p. 134

*September 29*

You cannot create a thing—not a
thought, an object, an event—no
experience of any kind—which is
outside of God's plan.

p. 61

*September 30*

I understand your fatigue. I know
you are tired of the struggle. Yet I
tell you this: When you follow Me
the struggle disappears.

p. 115

## October 1

You can choose to be a person
who has resulted simply from what
has happened, or from what
you've chosen to be and do about
what has happened.

p. 122

*October 2*

You cannot be ill without at some
level causing yourself to be, and
you can be well again in a moment
by simply deciding to be.

p. 32

*October 3*

In the moment you pledge your
highest love, you greet your
greatest fear.

p. 16

*October 4*

I talk to everyone. All the time. The
question is not to whom do I talk,
but who listens?

p. 3

*October 5*

Listen to your feelings. Listen to
your highest thoughts. Listen to
your experience. Whenever any of
these differ from what you've been
told by your teachers, or read in
your books, forget the words.
Words are the least reliable
purveyor of Truth.

p. 8

*October 6*

It is your soul's only desire to turn
its grandest concept about itself
into its greatest experience.

p. 22

By that which you call evil do you
define yourself—and by that which
you call good. The biggest evil
would therefore be to declare
nothing evil at all.

p. 134

*October 8*

When human love relationships
fail, they fail because they were
entered into for the wrong reason.

p. 122

*October 9*


A Master blesses calamity, for the
Master knows that from the seeds
of disaster (and all experience)
comes the growth of Self. And the
Master's . . . life purpose is always
growth.

p. 129

*October 10*

Life may more than once call upon
you to prove Who You Are by
demonstrating an aspect of Who
You Are Not.

p. 133

*October 11*

**All of you are special.**

p. 143

*October 12*

You must honor your feelings. For
honoring your feelings means
honoring your Self.

p. 128

*October 13*

A practicing Master does not speak
of suffering simply because a
Master practicing clearly
understands the power of the
Word—and so chooses to simply
not say a word about it.

p. 107

*October 14*

The soul is very clear that its
purpose is evolution. That is its
sole purpose—and its soul
purpose. It is not concerned with
the achievements of the body or
the development of the mind.
These are all meaningless to the
soul.

p. 82

*October 15*

Be watchful of the choices of
others, but not judgmental. Know
that their choice is perfect for them
in this moment now—yet stand
ready to assist them should the
moment come when they seek a
newer choice, a different choice—
a higher choice.

p. 47

*October 16*

You cannot move away from
something, because it will chase
you all over hell and back.
Therefore, resist not temptation—
but simply turn from it.

p. 104

*October 17*

You are a three-fold being. You
consist of body, mind and spirit.
You could also call these the
physical, the nonphysical and the
metaphysical. This is the Holy
Trinity, and it has been called by
many names.

p. 73

*October 18*

The truth is relentless. It won't
leave you alone. It keeps creeping
up on you from every side,
showing you what's really so.

p. 140

## October 19

If you do not go within, you go without.

p. 44

## October 20

It is a great challenge, this path of
the householder. There are many
distractions, many worldly
concerns. The aesthetic is bothered
by none of these. He is brought his
bread and water, and given his
humble mat on which to lie, and
he can devote his every hour to
prayer, meditation and
contemplation of the divine. How
easy to see the divine under such
circumstances! How simple a task!
Ah, but give one a spouse and
children!

## October 21

Some of you are walking in
wakefulness, and some of you are
sleepwalking. Yet all of you are
creating your own reality—
creating, not discovering.

p. 92

*October 22*

I have given you the tools with
which to respond and react to
events in a way which reduces—in
fact, eliminates—pain, but you
have not used them.

p. 105

*October 23*

Look to your experience to find
your truth.

p. 109

*October 24*

The point of life is not to get anywhere—it is to notice that you are, and have always been, already there.

p. 104

*October 25*

The Laws are very simple.

1. Thought is creative.
2. Fear attracts like energy.
3. Love is all there is.

p. 56

*October 26*

There is no such thing as an
incorrect path—for on this journey
you cannot "not get" where you
are going. It is simply a matter of
speed—merely a question of when
you will get there.

p. 104

*October* 27

The word of God was not a
commandment, but a covenant.

p. 95

*October 28*

What you open your eyes and look
at disappears. That is, it ceases to
hold its illusory form.

p. 102

*October 29*

All of your life you think you are
your body. Some of the time you
think you are your mind. It is at
the time of your death that you
find out Who You Really Are.

p. 81

*October 30*

The grandest teaching of Christ
was not that you shall have
everlasting life—but that you do.

p. 52

*October 31*

A true leader is not the one with
the most followers, but one who
creates the most leaders.

p. 114

## November 1

The realm of the relative was
created in order that I might
experience My Self. This does not
make the realm of the relative real.
It is a created reality you and I
have devised.

p. 56

*November 2*

If you cannot depend upon God's
love to always be there, on whose
love can you depend?

p. 16

## November 3

Feeling is the language of the soul.

p. 3

*November 4*

What you fear most is what will
most plague you. Fear will draw it
to you like a magnet.

p. 56

*November 5*

Joy, truth, love. These three are
interchangeable, and one always
leads to the other. It matters not in
which order they are placed.

p. 5

## November 6

My purpose will not be thwarted,
nor My will be ignored. You will
get the message. Sooner or later.

p. 5

*November 7*

What you resist persists.

p. 102

*November 8*

Do you imagine that a human soul
encounters life challenges—
whatever they may be—by
accident? Is this your imagining?

p. 45

*November 9*

Many people choose to believe
that God communicates in special
ways and only with special people.
This removes the mass of the
people from responsibility for
hearing My message . . . and allows
them to take someone else's word
for everything.

p. 6

## November 10

The original wisdom surrounding
suffering in silence has become so
perverted that now many believe
(and several religions actually
teach) that suffering is good, and
joy is bad.

p. 108

*November 11*

Words may help you understand
something. Experience allows you
to know.

p. 4

*November 12*

Nothing stays the same, nothing
remains static. Which way a thing
changes depends on you.

p. 79

*November 13*

From the beginning all man has
ever wanted is to love and be
loved. And from the beginning of
time man has done everything in
his power to make it impossible to
do that.

p. 208

*November 14*

You cannot be what you do not
know your Self to be.

p. 201

## November 15

You are telling me that you haven't
always gotten what you wanted.
Yet I am here to tell you that
you've always gotten what you
called forth. Your life is always a
result of your thoughts about it.

p. 118

*November 16*

You may do as you wish without
fear of retribution. It may serve
you, however, to be aware of
consequences. Consequences are
results. Natural outcomes. These
are not at all the same as
retributions or punishments.

p. 42

*November 17*

This is the greatest barrier to your
enlightenment: You think you
already know the truth! You think
you already understand how it is.
So you agree with everything that
falls into the paradigm of your
understanding, and reject
everything which does not. And
this you call learning.

*November 18*

Nothing occurs in your life—
nothing—which is not first a
thought. Thoughts are like
magnets, drawing effects to you.

p. 188

*November 19*

Everyone can love everything the
moment they understand what
they are doing, and why.

p. 186

*November 20*

A true teacher is not the one with
the most knowledge, but one who
causes the most others to have
knowledge.

p. 115

*November 21*

How can you think of wasting a
moment doing something for a
living you don't like to do? What
kind of a living is that? That is not
a living, that is a dying!

p. 185

*November 22*

Each to his own, without judgment—
that is the motto.

p. 206

*November 23*

Begin by being still. Quiet the
outer world, so that the inner
world might bring you sight.

**p. 44**

*November 24*

There is nothing you can't have if
you choose it. Even before you
ask, I will have given it to you.

p. 117

*November 25*

When body, mind and soul create
together, in harmony and in unity,
God is made flesh. Then does the
soul know itself in its own
experience. Then do the heavens
rejoice.

p. 175

*November 26*

The Holy Spirit will not force His
will upon your soul. It is outside of
the nature of the spirit to do so,
and thus, quite literally, impossible.

p. 175

*November 27*

Keep on deciding what you want
to become in the next highest
version of your Self. Keep on
working toward that. This is God
Work we're up to, You and I, so
keep on!

p. 158

*November 28*

There is no limit to what you can become.

p. 201

*November 29*

There are those who say that I
have given you free will, yet these
same people claim that if you do
not obey Me, I will send you to
hell. What kind of free will is that?

p. 39

*November 30*

Now is the time to go to your God
space more than ever.

p. 116

## December 1

If the entity which is you is to
create, and thus know, who it
really is, it must be through an act
of conscious volition, not an act of
unconscious obedience.

p. 175

*December 2*

Thankfulness is the most powerful
statement to God; an affirmation
that even before you ask, I have
answered. Therefore, never
supplicate, appreciate.

p. 11

## December 3

I tell you this: I am performing a
miracle right now.

p. 69

*December 4*

Every human thought, and every
human action, is based in either
love or fear. There is no other
human motivation.

p. 15

*December 5*

Be patient. You are gaining
wisdom.

p. 158

## December 6

I have given you a free will—the
power to do as you choose—and I
will never take that away from you,
ever.

p. 5

*December* 7

Go ahead and do what you really
love to do! Do nothing else!

p. 185

## December 8

All of your holy scriptures—of
every religious persuasion and
tradition—contain the clear
admonition: Fear not. Do you think
this is by accident?

p. 54

*December 9*

Life's irony is that as soon as world
goods and world success are of no
concern to you, the way is open
for them to flow to you.

p. 176

*December 10*

Are you going to be in a place
called fear, or in a place called
love? Where are you—and where
are you coming from—as you
encounter life?

p. 172

## December 11

Turn toward Me and away from
anything unlike Me.

p. 104

*December 12*

Bless every person and condition,
and give thanks. Thus you affirm
the perfection of God's creation—
and show your faith in it.

p. 46

*December 13*

Ultimately all Spirit renounces what
is not real, and nothing in the life
you lead is real, save your
relationship with Me.

p. 100

## December 14

The First Law is that you can be, do and have whatever you can imagine. The Second Law is that you attract what you fear.

p. 54

*December 15*

Suffering has nothing to do with
events, but with one's reaction to
them.

p. 105

*December 16*

The soul's decision precedes the
body's action in a highly conscious
person.

p. 185

*December 17*

In seeking to be Me, the soul has a
grand job ahead of it; an enormous.
menu of beingness from which to
choose. And that is what it is doing
in this moment now.

*December 18*

Religion is your attempt to speak
of the unspeakable. It does not do
a very good job.

p. 195

*December 19*

Nothing holy has ever been
achieved through denial. Yet
desires change as even larger
realities are glimpsed.

p. 206

*December 20*

What you actually experience is up
to you. It could be what you
planned to experience, or it could
be something else, depending
upon what you choose.

p. 174

*December 21*

You have this idea that God shows
up in only one way in life. That's a
very dangerous idea. It stops you
from seeing God all over.

p. 59

*December 22*

If a snowflake is utterly perfect in
its design, do you not think the
same could be said about
something as magnificent as your
life?

p. 46

*December 23*

No one does anything he doesn't
want to do.

p. 186

*December 24*

You are peace and joy and light.

p. 86

*December 25*

I have come to you, in this form,
right now, in answer to your call.

p. 7

*December 26*

The supreme irony here is that you
have all placed so much
importance on the Word of God,
and so little on the experience.

p. 4

*December 27*

You are, always and forever, in the
moment of pure creation.

p. 104

*December 28*

Joy and sacredness do mix (they
are, in fact, the same thing), and
many of you think that they do
not.

p. 207

*December 29*

You must first see yourself as
worthy before you can see another
as worthy. You must first see
yourself as blessed before you can
see another as blessed. You must
first know your Self to be holy
before you can acknowledge
holiness in another.

p. 126

## *December 30*

My Truth—and your surest help in
time of need—is as awesome as
the night sky, and as simply,
incontrovertibly, trustful as a baby's
gurgle. It is as loud as a pounding
heartbeat—and as quiet as a breath
taken in unity with Me.

p. 210

*December 31*

You want bells and whistles? I'll
see what I can arrange.

p. 59

# About the Artist

Louis Jones is a native of Tidewater, Virginia. His egg temperas, watercolors, and drawings reflect his love of nature and his love for people—capturing, as he describes, "the moving skies, the fluid landscapes, the hopes and dreams of all people, the heart and soul of humanity." Jones's work has been shown in galleries and museums throughout the United States and Europe, and he was one of the select American artists to display at the Contemporary Art Exhibit in Bath, England. He has also been included in *American Artists of Renown*.

For a limited edition of the original cover painting, *New Dawn*, by Louis Jones, please contact:

The Louis & Susan Jones Art Gallery
Dominion Tower, Suite 105
999 Waterside Drive
Norfolk, VA 23510

Phone: (757) 625-6505
Fax: (757) 499-5586
for further information

# NEALE DONALD WALSCH

## CONVERSATIONS WITH GOD BOOK 1

'Contains a wisdom I believe we all have inside us but don't stop to listen to ... There is the wisdom of the ages in this book'
Dr Bernie Siegel

**Suppose you could ask God the most puzzling questions about existence – questions about love and faith, life and death, good and evil.**

**Suppose God provided clear, understandable answers.**
**It happened to Neale Donald Walsch.**
*It can happen to you.*
**You are about to have a conversation ...**

Walsch was experiencing a low point in his life when he decided to write a letter to God, venting his frustrations. What he did not expect was a response. As he finished his letter, he was moved to continue writing – and out came these extraordinary answers to his questions.

They will amaze you with complex paradoxes that make perfect sense, profound logic, and astounding truths. Here are answers that bring together as one the deeper meaning of all beliefs and traditions. Here are answers that will change you, your life, and the way you view other beings.

For those with an open mind, a limitless curiosity, and a sincere desire to seek the truth, this book is stunning.

## HODDER AND STOUGHTON PAPERBACKS

# NEALE DONALD WALSCH

## CONVERSATIONS WITH GOD BOOK 2

**The dialogue continues …**

… this paradigm shift will take great wisdom, great courage, and massive determination. For fear will strike at the heart of these concepts, and call them false. Fear will eat at the core of these magnificent truths, and make them appear hollow …

Yet you will not have, cannot produce, the society of which you have always dreamed unless and until you see with wisdom and clarity the ultimate truth: that what you do to others, you do to yourself; what you fail to do for others, you fail to do for yourself; that the pain of others is your pain, and the joy of others your joy, and that when you disclaim any part of it, you disclaim a part of yourself.

Now is the time to *reclaim yourself.* Now is the time to see yourself again as Who You Really Are, and thus, render yourself visible again. For when you, and your true relationship with God, become visible, then We are *indivisible.*

And nothing will ever divide Us again.

HODDER AND STOUGHTON PAPERBACKS

**NEALE DONALD WALSCH**

## CONVERSATIONS WITH GOD BOOK 3

**The dialogue expands ...**

You are always a part *of* God, because you are never
apart *from* God.

This is the truth of your being. We are Whole.
So now you know the whole truth.

This truth has been food for the hungry soul.
Take, and eat it. The world has thirsted for this joy.
Take, and drink of it. Do this in re-membrance of Me.

For truth is the body, and joy is the blood, of God,
who is love.

> Truth.
> Joy.
> Love.

These three are interchangeable. One leads to the other, and it
matters not in which order they appear. All lead to Me.
All *are* Me.

And so I end this dialogue as it began. As with life itself, it comes
full circle. You have been given truth here. You have been given
joy. You have been given love. You have been given here the
answers to the largest mysteries of life. There is now only one
question remaining. It is the question with which we began.

The question is not, to whom do I talk, but who listens?

HODDER AND STOUGHTON PAPERBACKS

# A selection of bestsellers from
# Hodder & Stoughton

| | | | | |
|---|---|---|---|---|
| Conversations with God Book 1 | | 0 340 69325 8 | £7.99 | ☐ |
| Conversations with God Book 2 | | 0 340 76544 5 | £7.99 | ☐ |
| Conversations with God Book 3 | | 0 340 76545 3 | £7.99 | ☐ |
| Ishmael | David Quinn | 0 340 71710 6 | £9.99 | ☐ |
| My Ishmael | David Quinn | 0 340 71711 4 | £9.99 | ☐ |

*All Hodder & Stoughton books are available at your local bookshop or newsagent, or can be ordered direct from the publisher. Just tick the titles you want and fill in the form below. Prices and availability subject to change without notice.*

Hodder & Stoughton Books, Cash Sales Department, Bookpoint, 39 Milton Park, Abingdon, OXON, OX14 4TD, UK. E-mail address: order@bookpoint.co.uk. If you have a credit card you may order by telephone – (01235) 400414.

Please enclose a cheque or postal order made payable to Bookpoint Ltd to the value of the cover price and allow the following for postage and packing:
UK & BFPO – £1.00 for the first book, 50p for the second book, and 30p for each additional book ordered up to a maximum charge of £3.00.
OVERSEAS & EIRE – £2.00 for the first book, £1.00 for the second book, and 50p for each additional book

Name .................................................................................

Address ............................................................................

............................................................................................

............................................................................................

If you would prefer to pay by credit card, please complete:
Please debit my Visa/Access/Diner's Card/American Express (delete as applicable) card no:

| | | | | | | | | | | | | | | | | |
|--|--|--|--|--|--|--|--|--|--|--|--|--|--|--|--|--|

Signature .........................................................................

Expiry Date .....................................................................

If you would NOT like to receive further information on our products please tick the box. ☐